T0066184

ADELE 25

EASY GUITAR WITH NOTES & TAB

ISBN 978-1-4950-5811-0

HAL•LEONARD® CORPORATION

7777 W. BLUEMOUND RD. P.O. BOX 13819 MILWAUKEE, WI 53213

Visit Hal Leonard Online at
www.halleonard.com

STRUM AND PICK PATTERNS

This chart contains the suggested strum and pick patterns that are referred to by number at the beginning
of each song in this book. The symbols ⊓ and ∨ in the strum patterns refer to down and up strokes, respectively.
The letters in the pick patterns indicate which right-hand fingers play which strings.

p = thumb
i = index finger
m = middle finger
a = ring finger

For example; Pick Pattern 2
is played: thumb - index - middle - ring

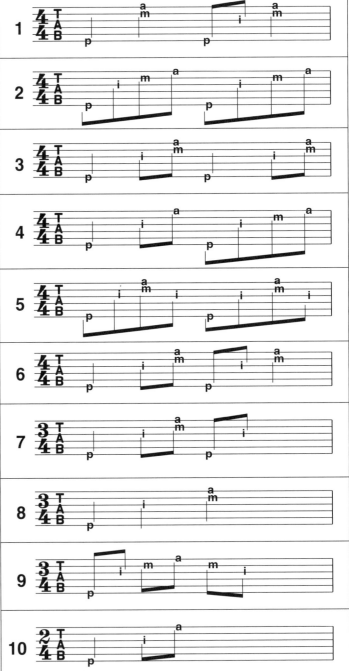

Strum Patterns

Pick Patterns

You can use the 3/4 Strum and Pick Patterns in songs written in compound meter (6/8, 9/8, 12/8, etc.).
For example, you can accompany a song in 6/8 by playing the 3/4 pattern twice in each measure.
The 4/4 Strum and Pick Patterns can be used for songs written in cut time (¢) by doubling the note
time values in the patterns. Each pattern would therefore last two measures in cut time.

Hello

Words and Music by Adele Adkins and Greg Kurstin

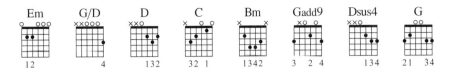

*Capo I

Strum Pattern: 6
Pick Pattern: 6

Intro
Moderately slow

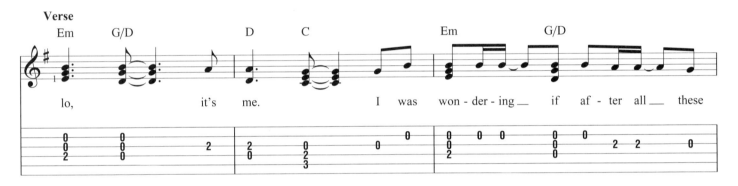

*Optional: To match recording, place capo at 1st fret.

Verse

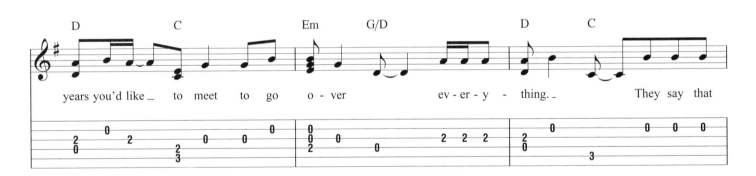

lo,   it's me.   I was won- der- ing ___ if af- ter all ___ these

years you'd like ___ to meet to go o- ver   ev- er- y - thing. ___ They say that

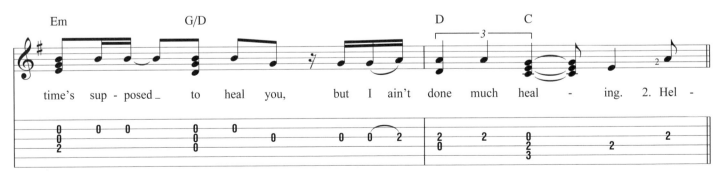

time's sup- posed ___ to heal you,   but I ain't done much heal - ing. 2. Hel -

Verse

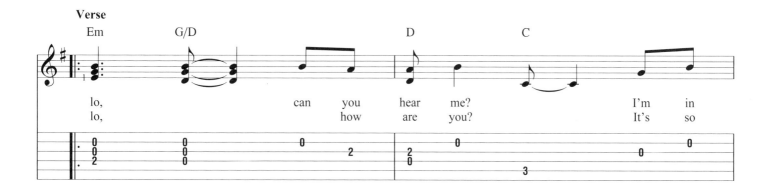

Pre-Chorus

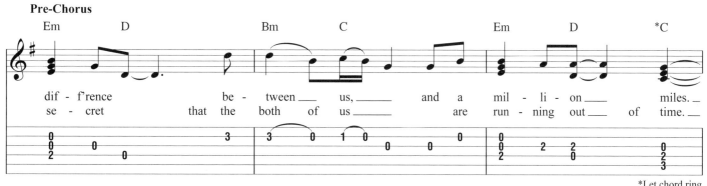

𝄋 Chorus

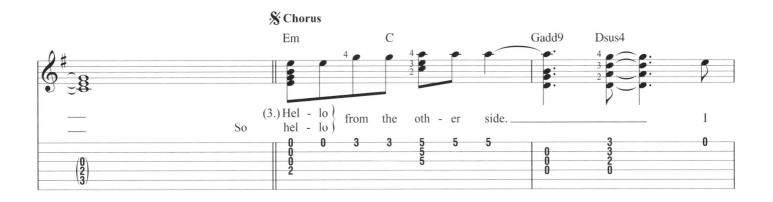

So (3.)Hel - lo / from the oth - er side. _____ I
So hel - lo \

must have called a thou-sand times _____ to tell you _____ I'm sor - ry for ev-'ry-

*Sung one octave higher.

thing that I've done, _ but when I call, _____ you nev - er seem to be home. _

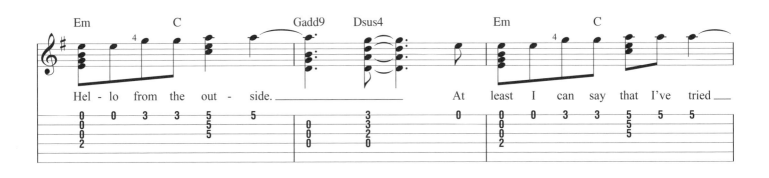

Hel - lo from the out - side. _____ At least I can say that I've tried _____

_____ to tell you _____ I'm sor - ry for break-ing your heart. But it don't mat -

6

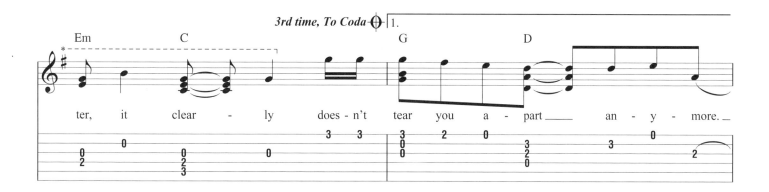

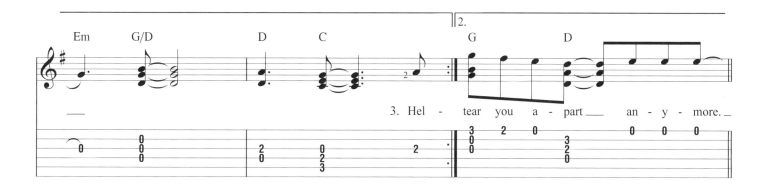

Interlude

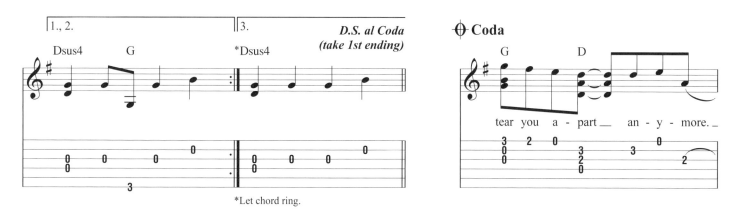

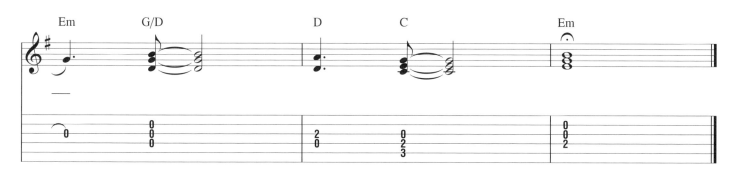

Send My Love (To Your New Lover)

Words and Music by Adele Adkins, Max Martin and Shellback

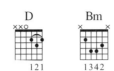

Strum Pattern: 1
Pick Pattern: 1

Intro
Moderately slow

*Chord symbols reflect implied harmony.

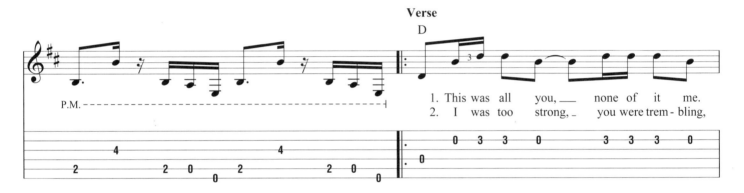

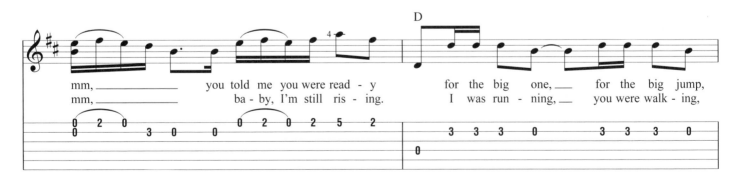

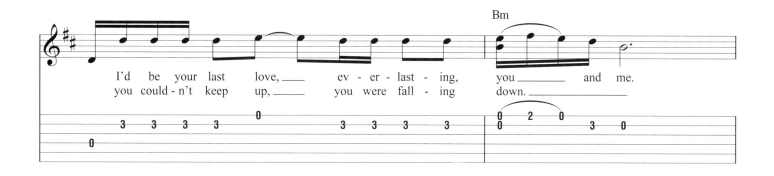

I'd be your last love, _____ ev - er - last - ing, you _____ and me.
you could - n't keep up, _____ you were fall - ing down. _____

Pre-Chorus

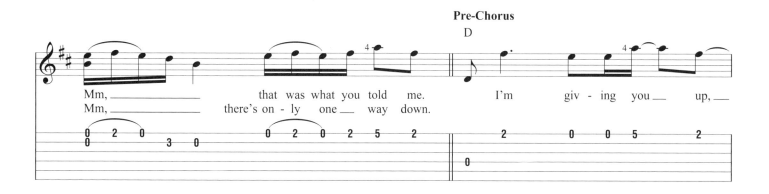

Mm, _____ that was what you told me. I'm giv - ing you _____ up, _____
Mm, _____ there's on - ly one _____ way down.

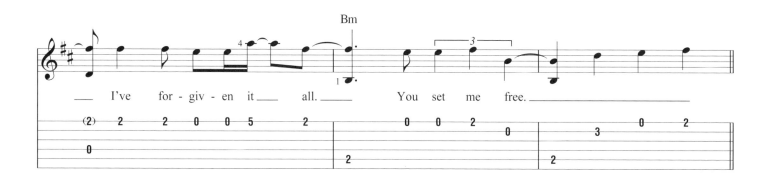

_____ I've for - giv - en it _____ all. _____ You set me free. _____

𝄋 Chorus

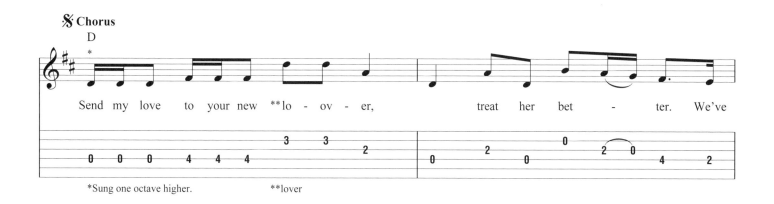

Send my love to your new **lo - ov - er, treat her bet - ter. We've

*Sung one octave higher.   **lover

got - ta let go of all of our ghosts. We both know we ain't kids no more. _____

Send my love to your new lo - ov - er, treat her bet - ter. We've

3rd time, To Coda ⊕

got - ta let go of all of our ghosts. We both know we ain't kids no more. _____

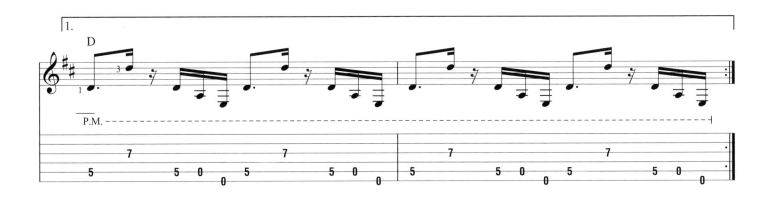

1.

_____ If you're read - y, _____ if you're read - y,

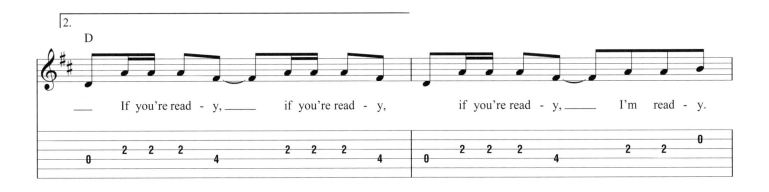

2.

if you're read - y, _____ I'm read - y.

If you're read - y, _____ if you're read - y, we both know we ain't kids no more. _____

Interlude
w/ Lead Voc. ad lib.

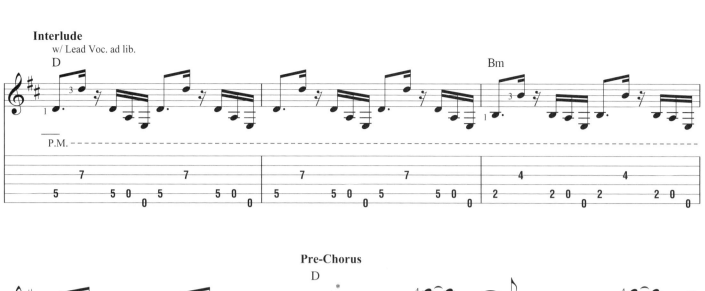

I'm giv-ing you up, I've for-giv-en it all.

*Sung as written.

Coda

D.S. al Coda

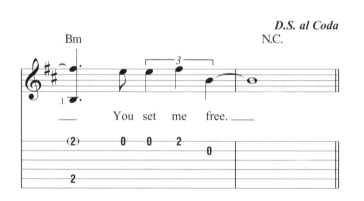

You set me free.

Outro

If you're read-y, if you're read-y,

if you're read-y, I'm read-y. Got-ta let go of all of our ghosts.

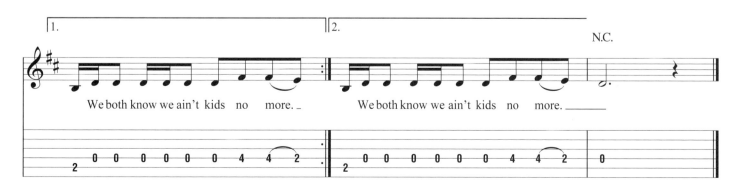

We both know we ain't kids no more.   *We both know we ain't kids no more.*

I Miss You

Words and Music by Adele Adkins and Paul Epworth

*Capo III

Strum Pattern: 3
Pick Pattern: 3

Intro
Moderately

*Optional: To match recording, place capo at 3rd fret.

**Chord symbols reflect implied harmony.

1. I want ev-'ry sin-gle piece of you, _____ I want your heav-en and your o-ceans too.
2. I love the way your bod-y moves _____ to-wards me from a-cross the room, _____

_____ Treat me soft but touch me cool, _____ I wan-na teach you things you nev-er knew, _____
brush-ing past my ev-'ry groove. _____ No one has me like you do, _____

Pre-Chorus

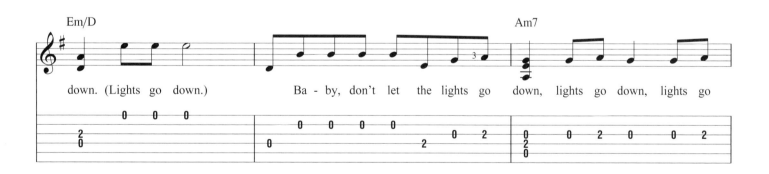

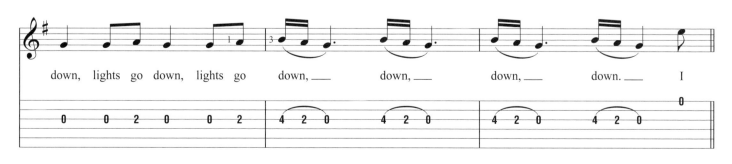

%. **Chorus**

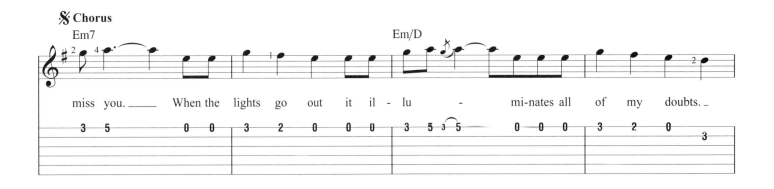

miss you. ____ When the lights go out it il - lu - mi-nates all of my doubts. ____

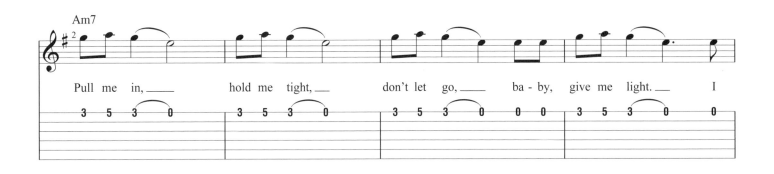

Pull me in, ____ hold me tight, __ don't let go, ____ ba - by, give me light. __ I

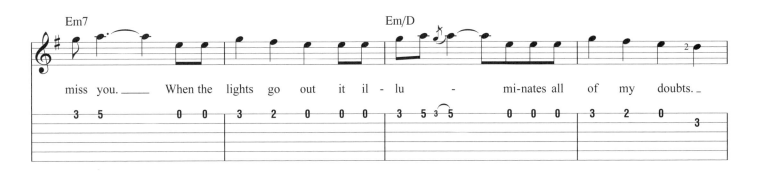

miss you. ____ When the lights go out it il - lu - mi-nates all of my doubts. __

2nd time, To Coda 1 ⊕
3rd time, To Coda 2 ⊕

D.C. al Coda 1
(take 2nd ending)

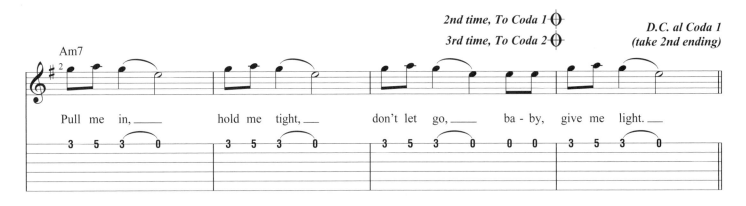

Pull me in, ____ hold me tight, __ don't let go, ____ ba - by, give me light. __

⊕ **Coda 1** **Bridge**

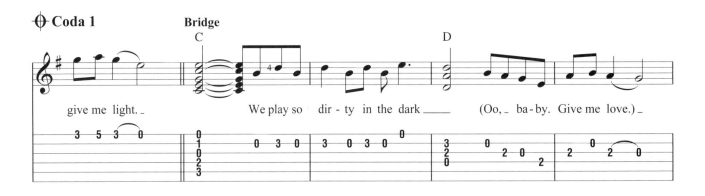

give me light. __ We play so dir - ty in the dark ____ (Oo, _ ba - by. Give me love.) __

When We Were Young

Words and Music by Adele Adkins and Tobias Jesso Jr.

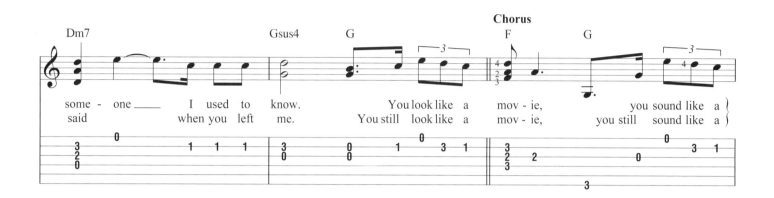

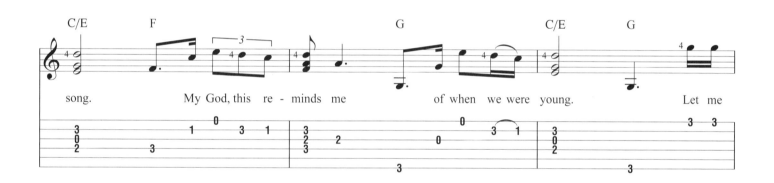

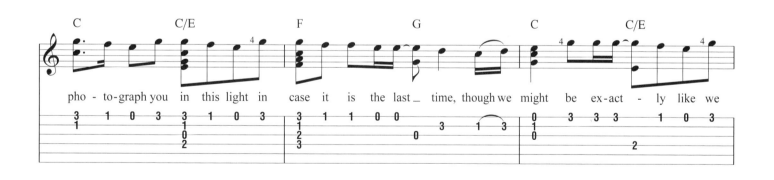

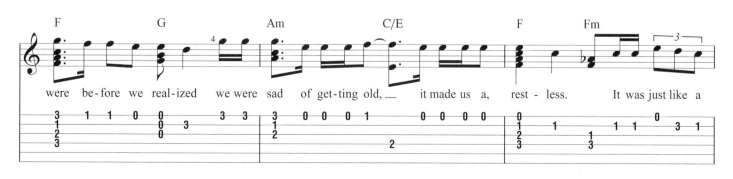

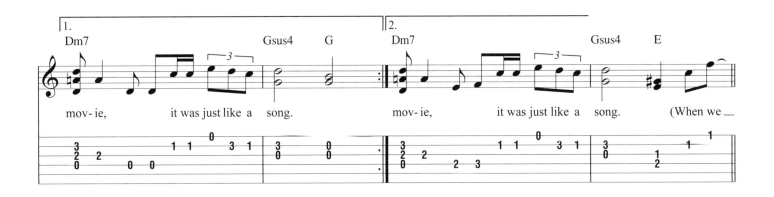

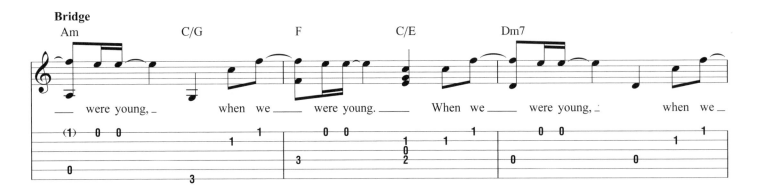

Bridge

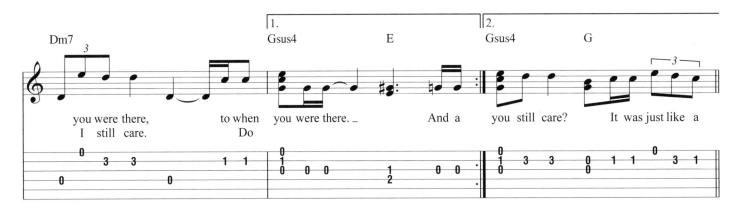

Chorus

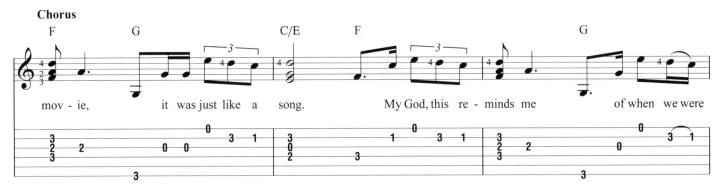

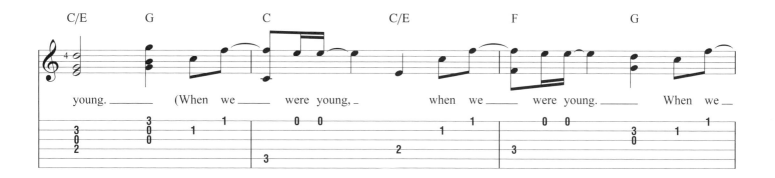

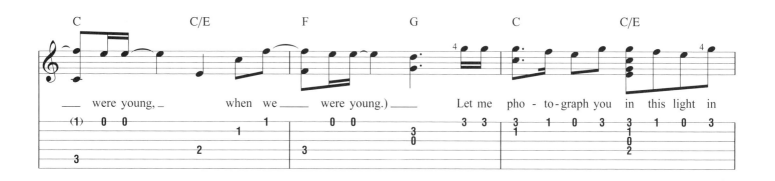

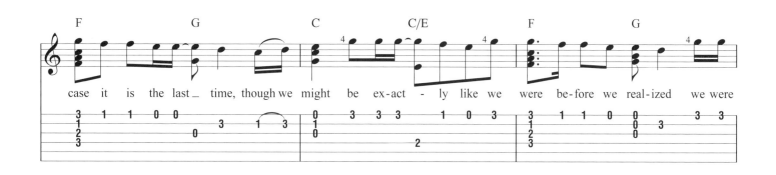

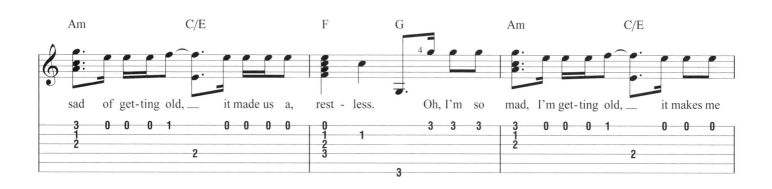

Remedy

Words and Music by Adele Adkins and Ryan Tedder

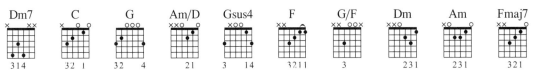

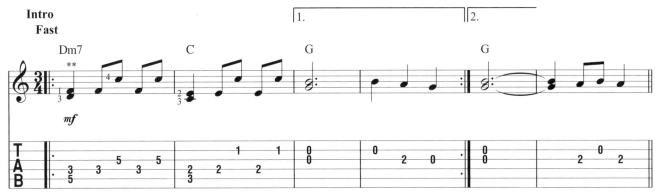

*Capo II

Strum Pattern: 7
Pick Pattern: 7

Intro
Fast

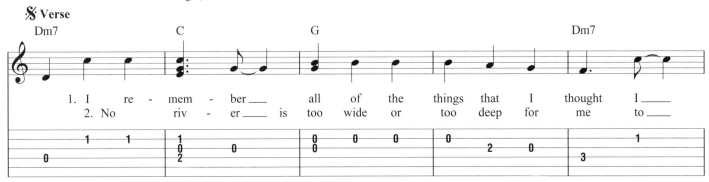

*Optional: To match recording, place capo at 2nd fret.

**Piano arr. for gtr., next 6 meas.

% **Verse**

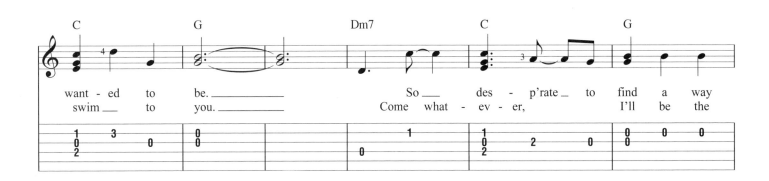

1. I re-mem-ber ___ all of the things that I thought I ___
2. No riv-er ___ is too wide or too deep for me to ___

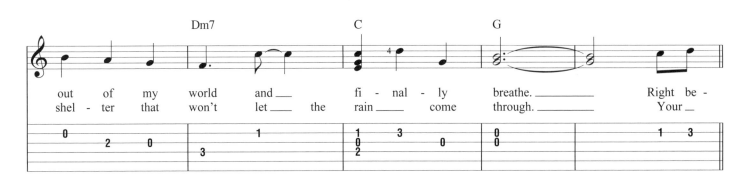

want-ed to be. ___ So ___ des-p'rate ___ to find a way
swim ___ to you. ___ Come what-ev-er, I'll be the

out of my world and ___ fi-nal-ly breathe. ___ Right be-
shel-ter that world won't let ___ the rain come through. ___ Your ___

Pre-Chorus

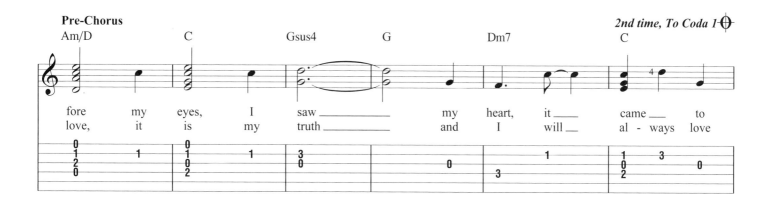

fore   my   eyes,   I   saw _____ my   heart,   it _____ came ____ to

love,   it   is   my   truth _____ and   I   will ____ al - ways love

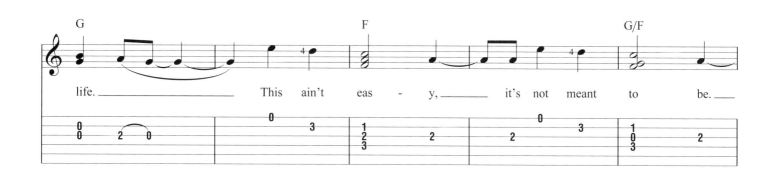

life. _____ This   ain't   eas -   y, _____ it's   not   meant   to   be. ____

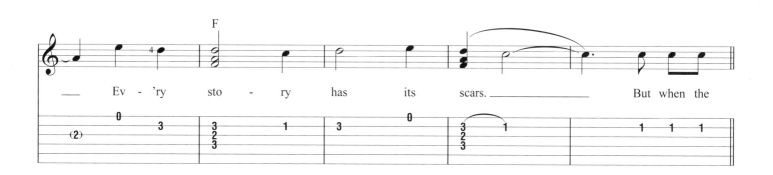

____ Ev - 'ry   sto -   ry   has   its   scars. _____ But when the

𝄋 𝄋 Chorus

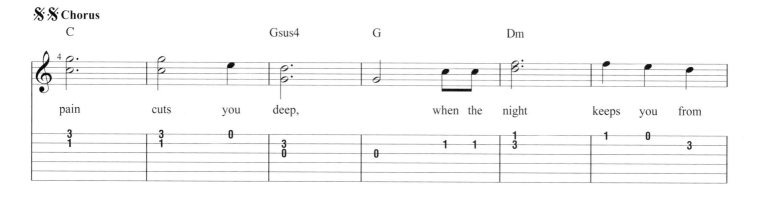

pain   cuts   you   deep,   when   the   night   keeps   you   from

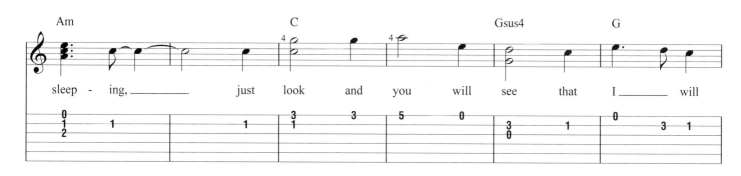

sleep - ing, _____ just   look   and   you   will   see   that   I _____ will

Coda 2

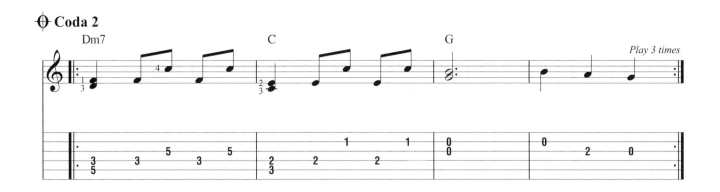

D.S.S. al Coda 3

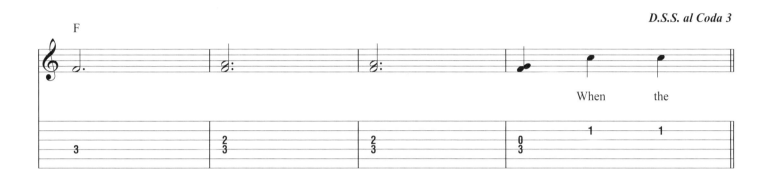

Coda 3

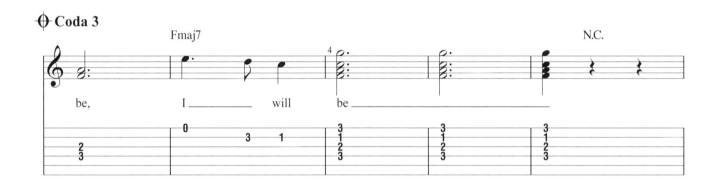

Outro

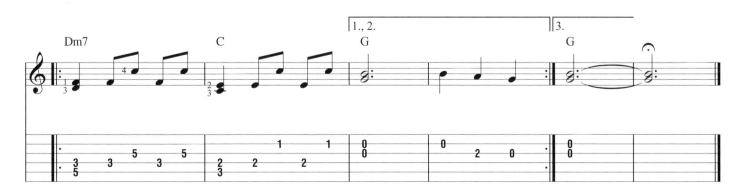

Water Under the Bridge

Words and Music by Adele Adkins and Gregory Kurstin

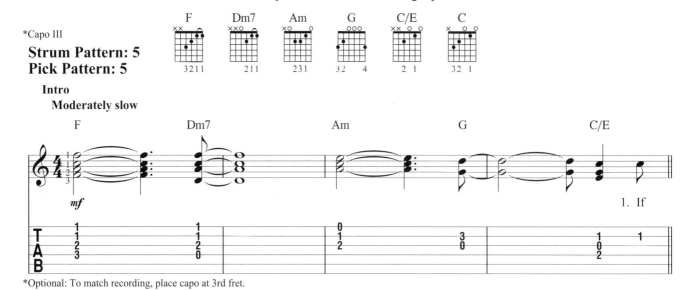

*Capo III

Strum Pattern: 5
Pick Pattern: 5

Intro
Moderately slow

*Optional: To match recording, place capo at 3rd fret.

Verse

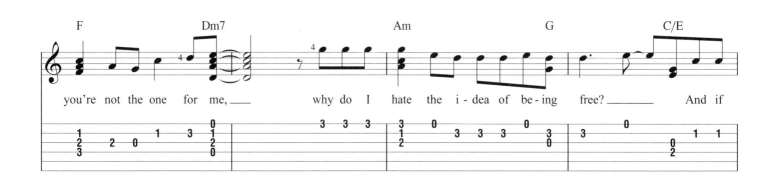

you're not the one for me, _____ then I'll come, I can bring you to your knees. _____ If

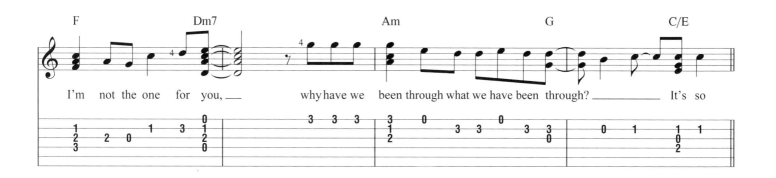

I'm not the one for you, ___ why have we been through what we have been through? ___ It's so

Pre-Chorus

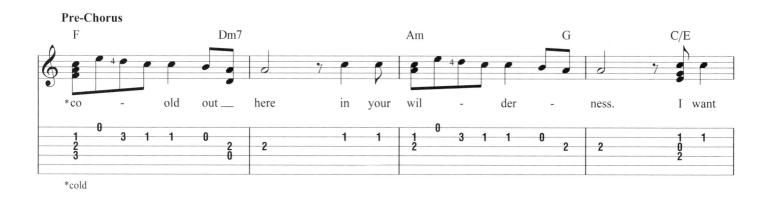

*co - old out ___ here in your wil - der - ness. I want

*cold

you ___ to be my keep - er, but not if you are so reck - less. ___ If you're gon-na

Chorus

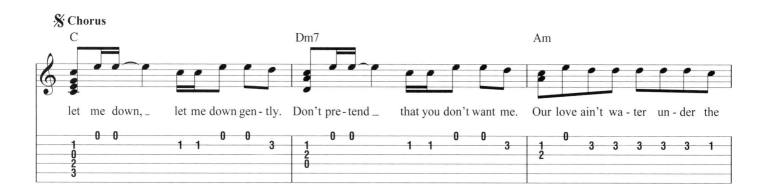

let me down, _ let me down gen - tly. Don't pre - tend _ that you don't want me. Our love ain't wa - ter un - der the

bridge. If you're gon-na let me down, _ let me down gen - tly. Don't pre - tend _ that you don't want me.

Our love ain't wa-ter un-der the bridge. Oh, ___ whoa, ___

2nd time, To Coda 1
3rd time, To Coda 2

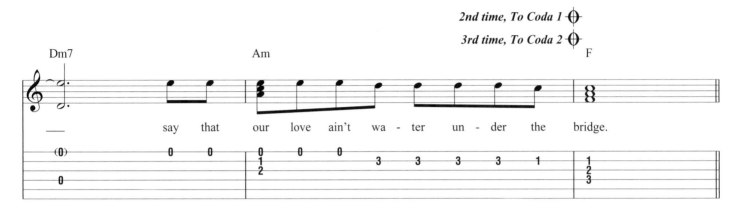

___ say that our love ain't wa-ter un-der the bridge.

Verse

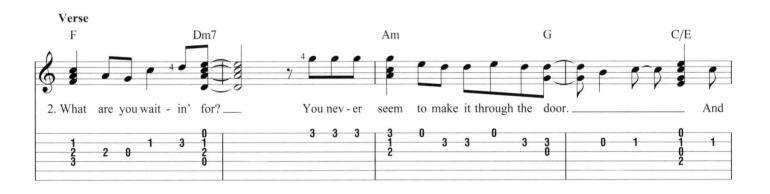

2. What are you wait-in' for? ___ You nev-er seem to make it through the door. ___ And

who are you hid-in' from? ___ It ain't no life to live like you're on the run. ___ Have

D.S. al Coda 1

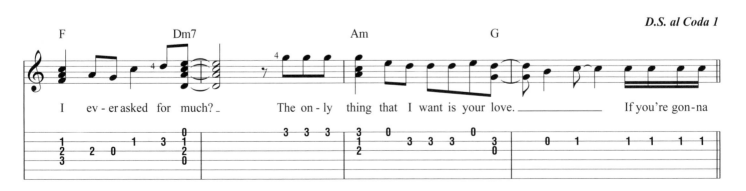

I ev-er asked for much? _ The on-ly thing that I want is your love. ___ If you're gon-na

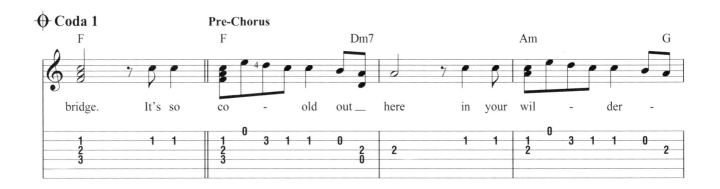

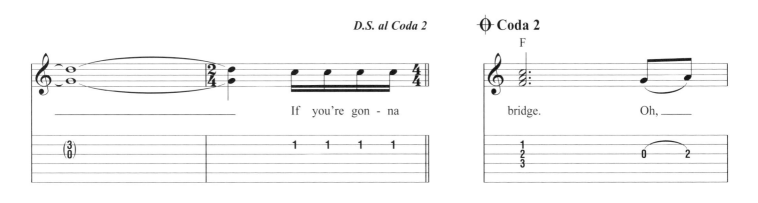

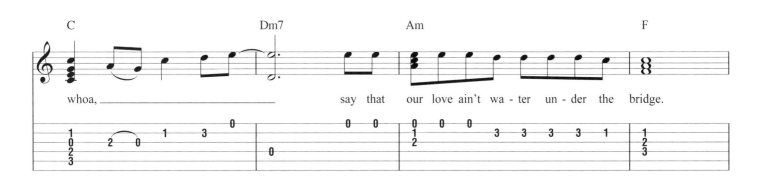

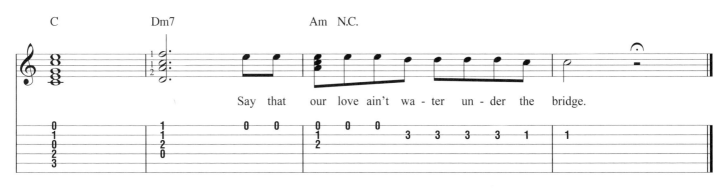

River Lea

Words and Music by Adele Adkins and Brian Burton

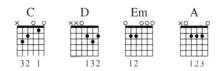

*Tune down 1/2 step:
(low to high): E♭-A♭-D♭-G♭-B♭-E♭

Strum Pattern: 3
Pick Pattern: 3

Intro
Moderately slow, in 2

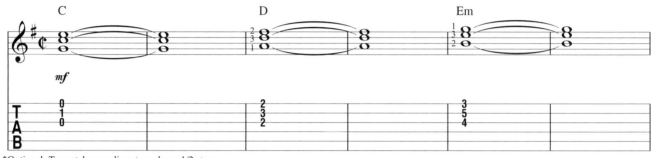

*Optional: To match recording, tune down 1/2 step.

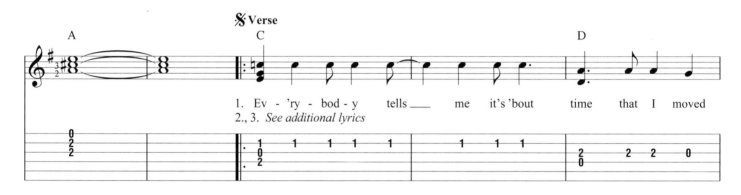

1. Ev - 'ry - bod - y tells ___ me it's 'bout time that I moved
2., 3. *See additional lyrics*

on and I need to learn ___ to light - en up and learn how to be young. ___ But

my heart is a val - ley, it's so shal - low and man - made. I'm scared to death ___ if I

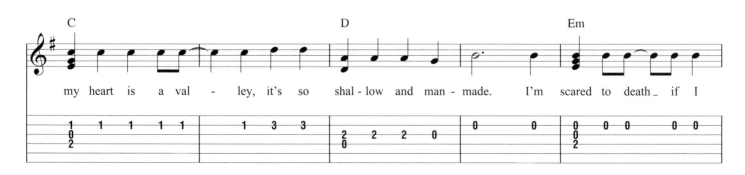

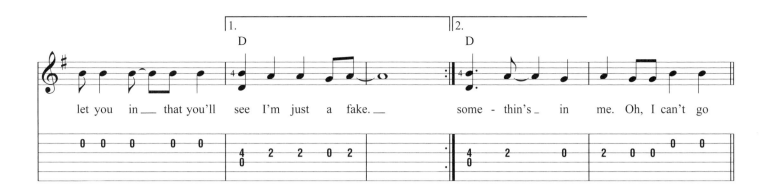

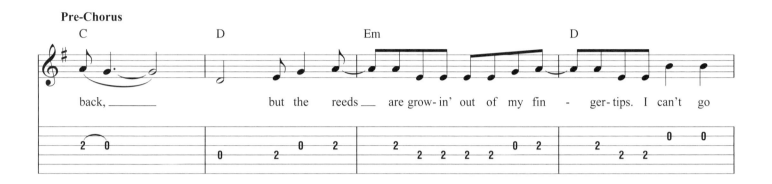

Pre-Chorus

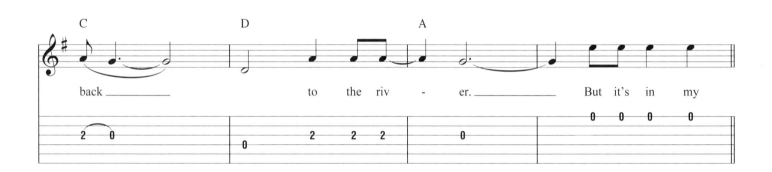

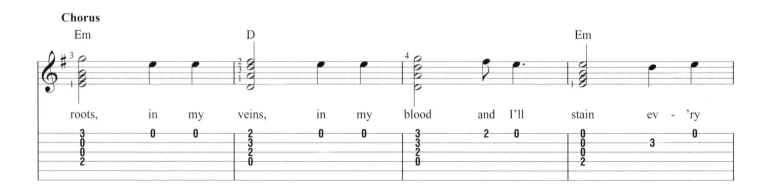

Chorus

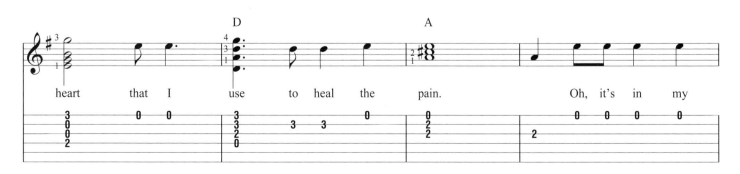

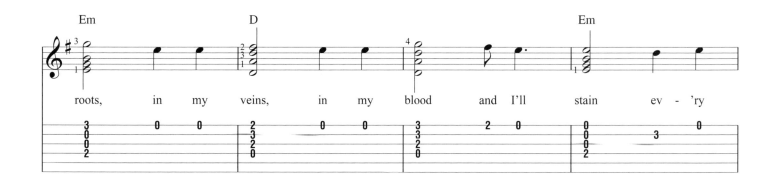

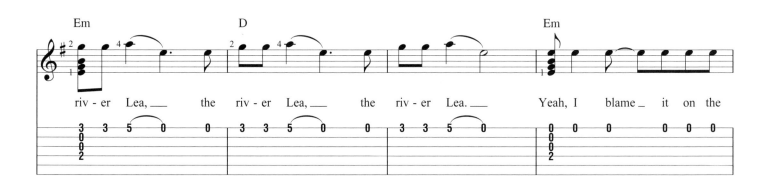

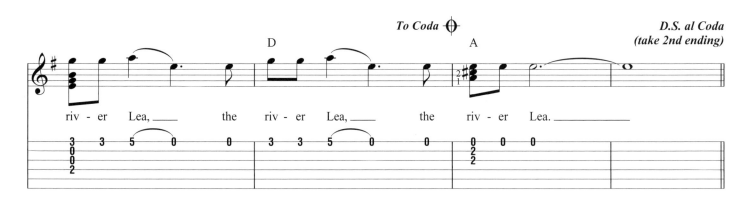

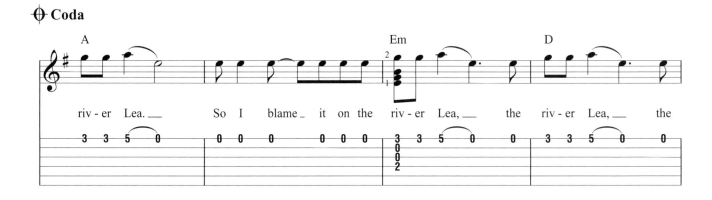

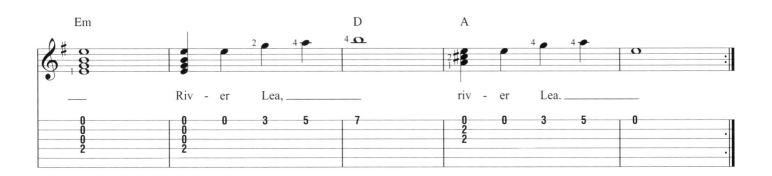

Additional Lyrics

2. Sometimes I feel lonely in the arms of your touch,
   But I know that's just me 'cause nothing ever is enough.
   When I was a child I grew up by the river Lea,
   And there was somethin' in the water; now that somethin's in me.
   Oh, I can't go back...

3. I should prob'ly tell you now before it's way too late
   That I never meant to hurt you or to lie straight to your face.
   Consider this my apology, I know it's years in advance,
   But I would rather say it now in case I never get the chance.
   No, I can't go back...

Love in the Dark

Words and Music by Adele Adkins and Samuel Dixon

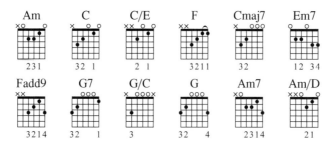

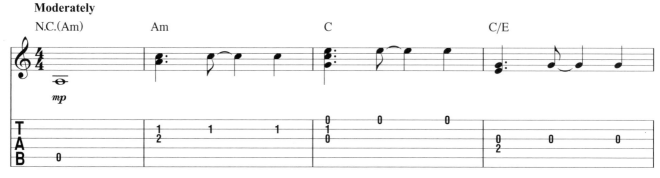

Strum Pattern: 6
Pick Pattern: 6

Intro
Moderately

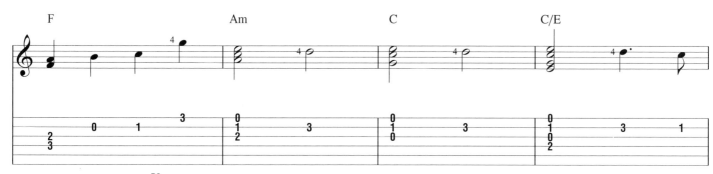

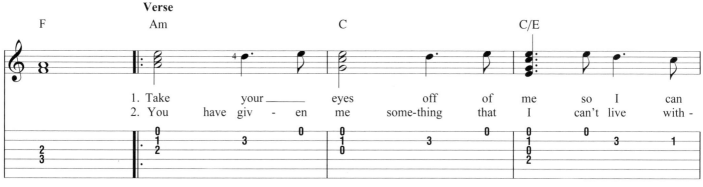

1. Take your _____ eyes off of me so I can
2. You have giv - en me some-thing that I can't live with -

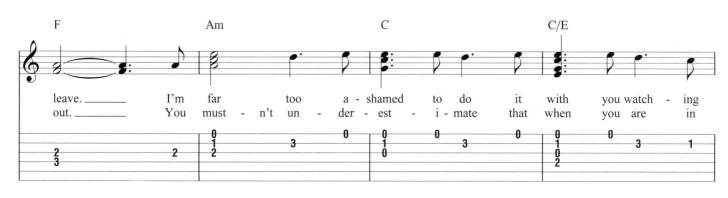

leave. _____ I'm far too a - shamed to do it with you watch - ing
out. _____ You must - n't un - der - est - i - mate that when you are in

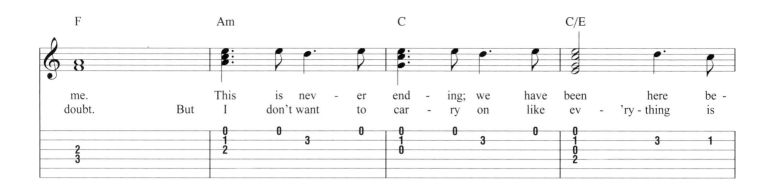

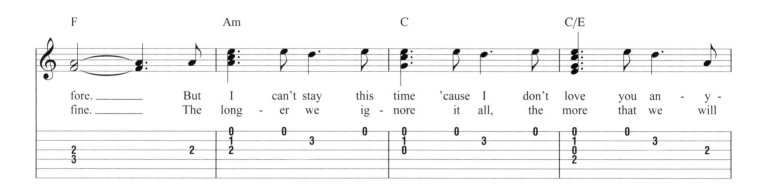

Pre-Chorus

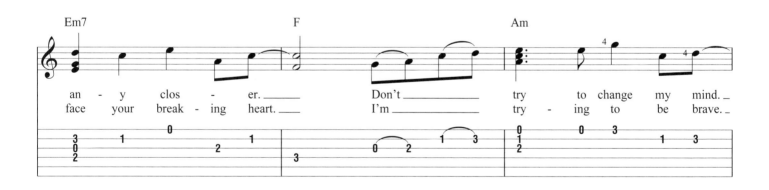

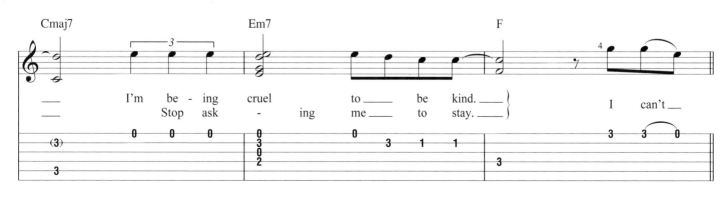

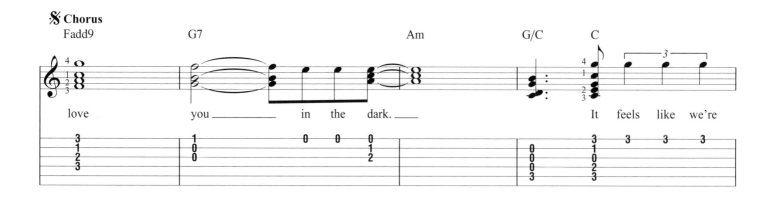

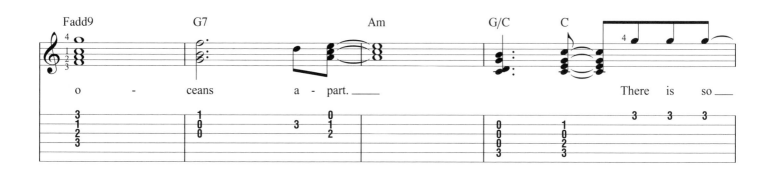

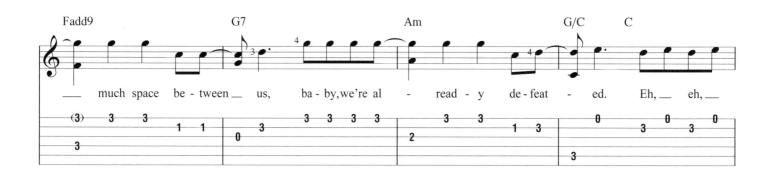

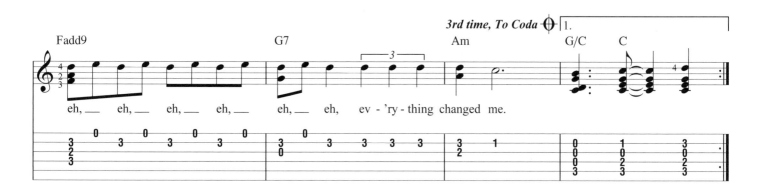

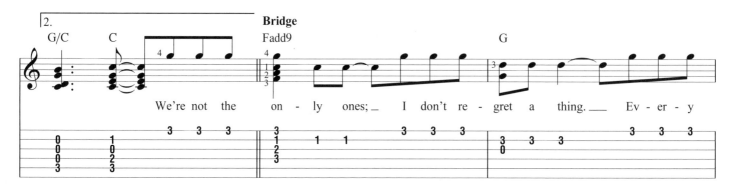

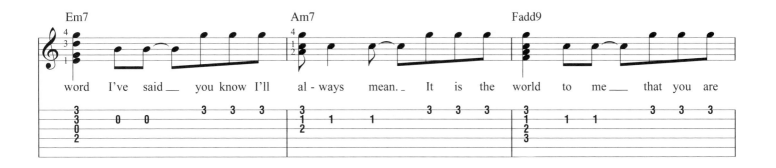

word I've said ___ you know I'll al - ways mean. ___ It is the world to me ___ that you are

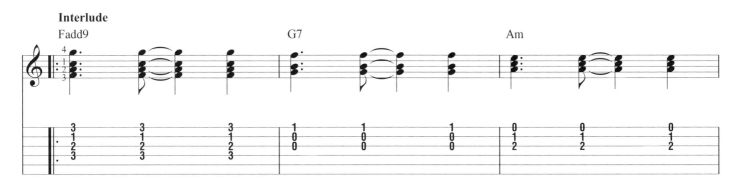

in my life, ___ but I want ___ to live ___ and not ___ just sur - vive. ___

Interlude

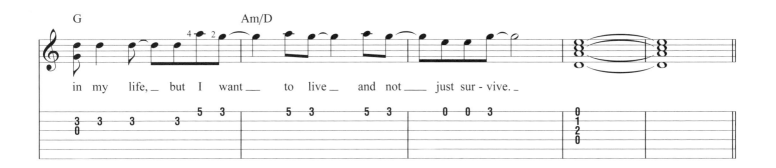

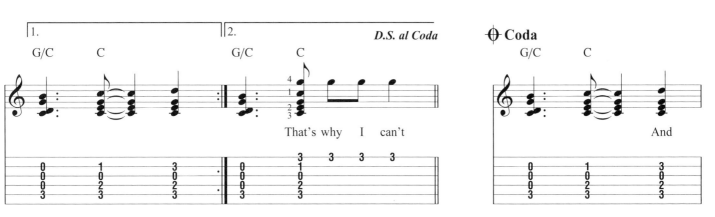

That's why I can't

And

Freely

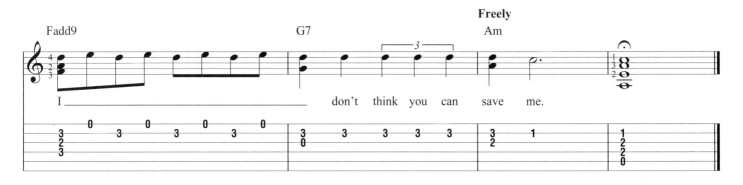

I ___ don't think you can save me.

Million Years Ago

Words and Music by Adele Adkins and Gregory Kurstin

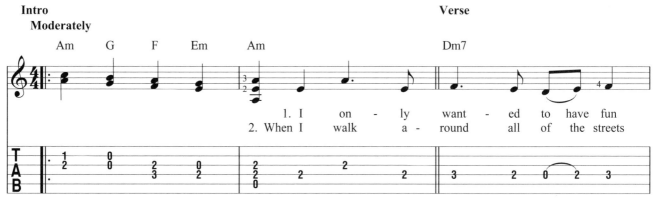

*Capo IV

Strum Pattern: 6
Pick Pattern: 6

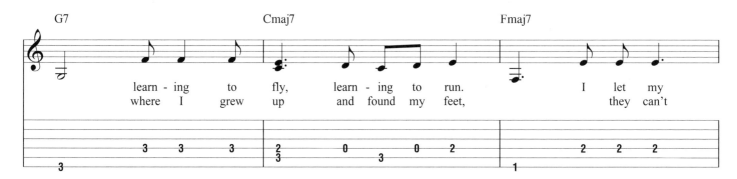

Intro
Moderately

Verse

1. I on - ly want - ed to have fun
2. When I walk a - round all of the streets

*Optional: To match recording, place capo at 4th fret.

learn - ing to fly, learn - ing to run.
where I grew up and found my feet,

I let my
they can't

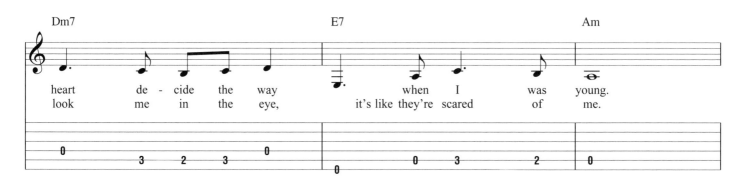

heart de - cide the way
look me in the eye,

when I was young.
it's like they're scared of me.

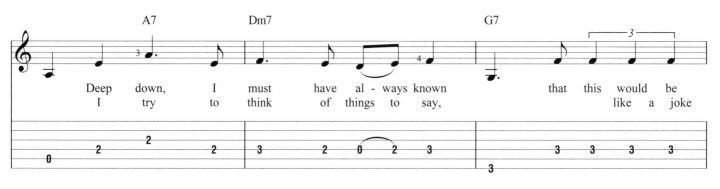

Deep down, I must have al - ways known
I try to think of things to say,

that this would be
like a joke

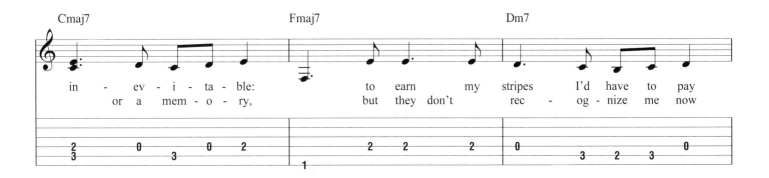

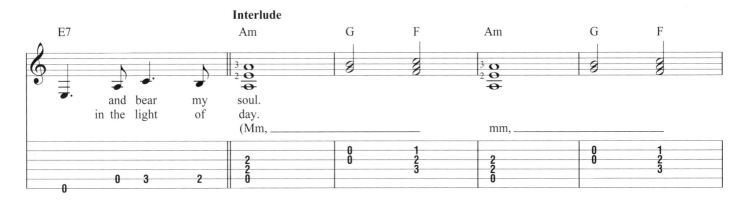

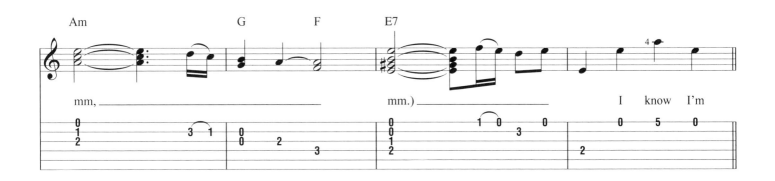

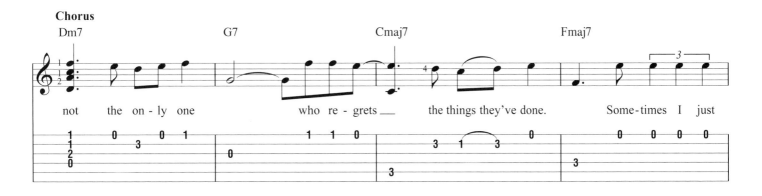

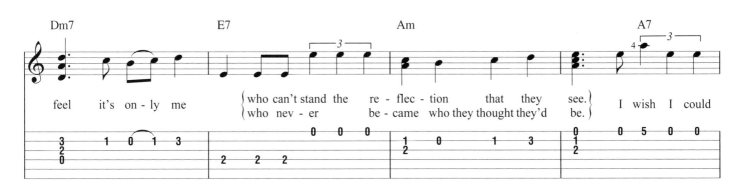

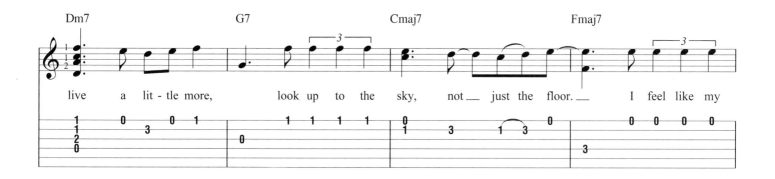

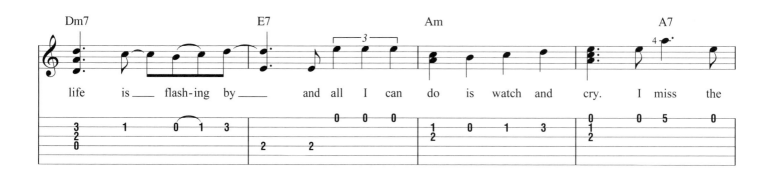

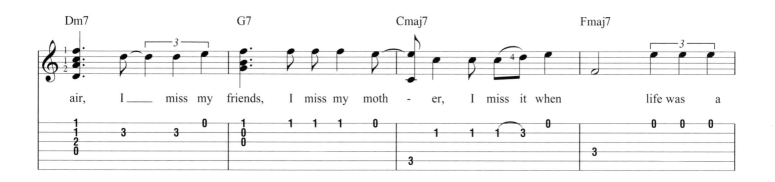

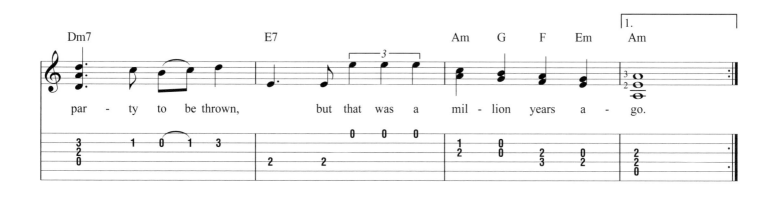

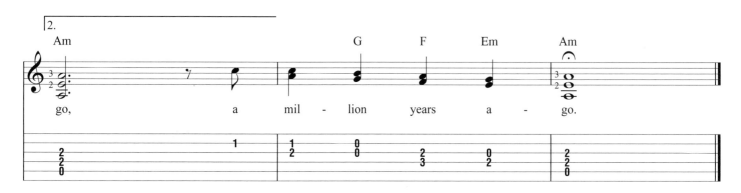

All I Ask

Words and Music by Adele Adkins, Philip Lawrence, Bruno Mars and Chris Brown

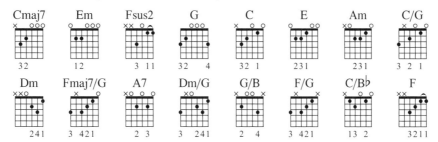

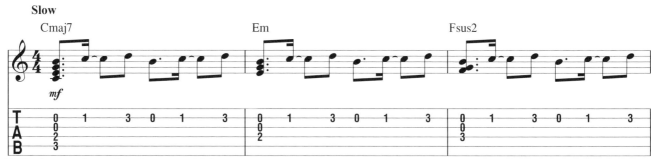

*Capo IV

Strum Pattern: 3
Pick Pattern: 5

*Optional: To match recording, place capo at 4th fret.

1. I will leave _ my heart at the door. _ I won't
2. I don't need _ your hon-es-ty _ it's al-read-y

say a word. _ They've all been said be-fore, _ you know, _ so why don't we _____ just
in your eyes _ and I'm sure my eyes, they speak _ for me. _____ No one knows _____ me

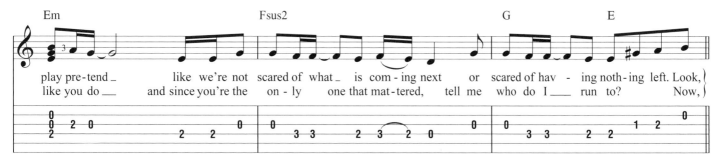

play pre-tend _ like we're not scared of what _ is com-ing next or scared of hav-ing noth-ing left. Look,
like you do _ and since you're the on-ly one that mat-tered, tell me who do I _____ run to? Now,

Pre-Chorus

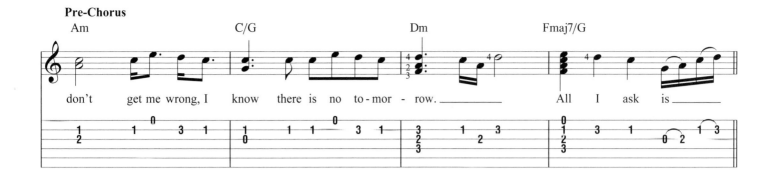

don't get me wrong, I know there is no to-mor-row. _____ All I ask is _____

𝄋 Chorus

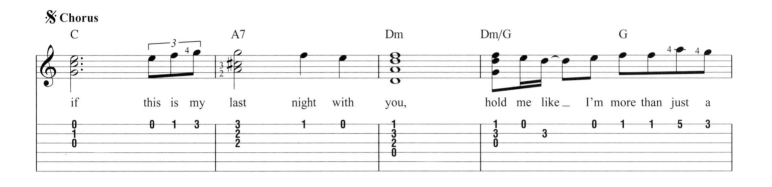

if this is my last night with you, hold me like _ I'm more than just a

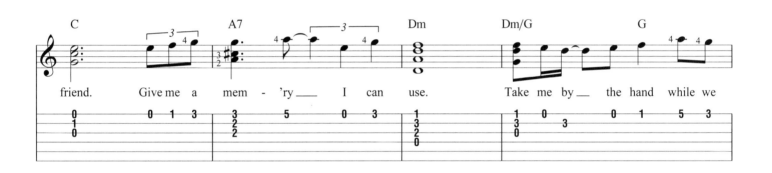

friend. Give me a mem - 'ry _____ I can use. Take me by __ the hand while we

3rd time, To Coda 𝄌

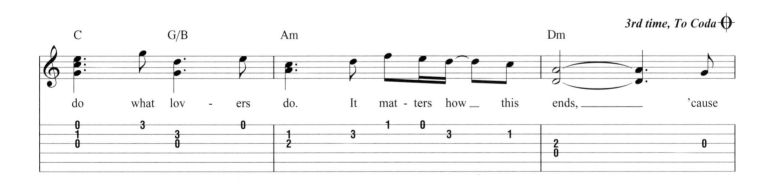

do what lov - ers do. It mat - ters how _ this ends, _____ 'cause

1.

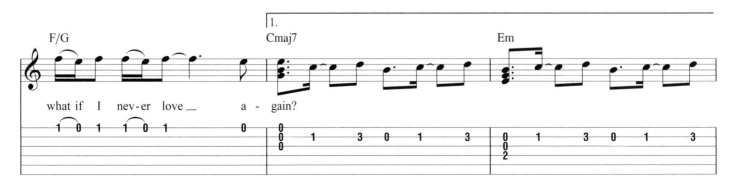

what if I nev-er love _ a - gain?

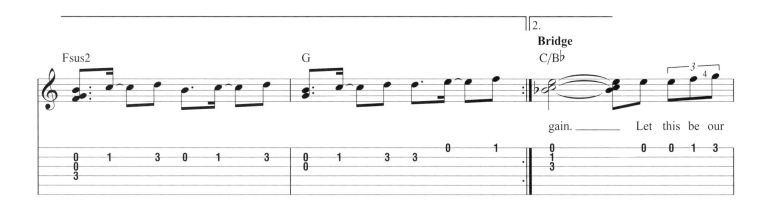

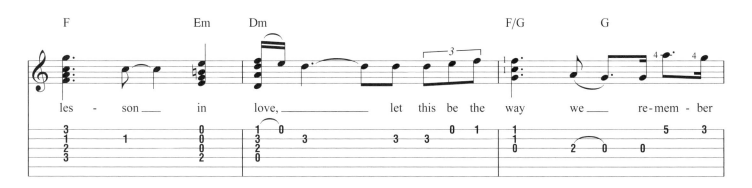

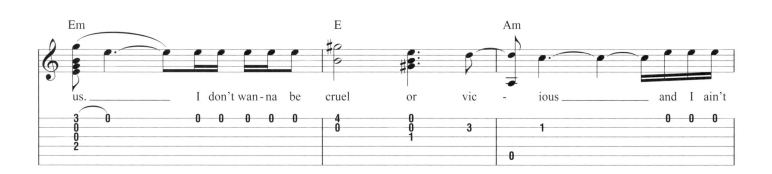

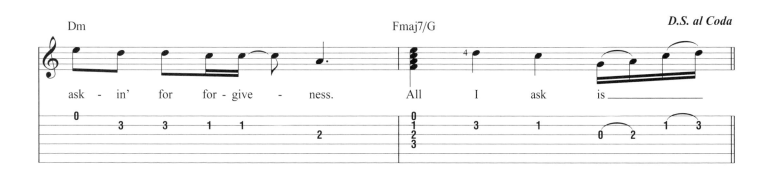

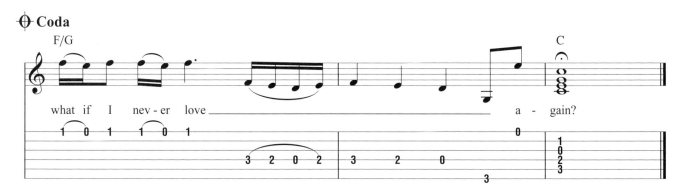

Sweetest Devotion

Words and Music by Adele Adkins and Paul Epworth

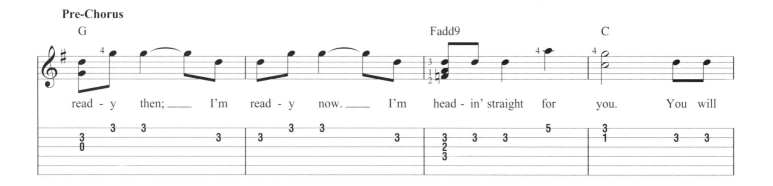

ready then;____ I'm ready now.____ I'm headin' straight for you.____ You will

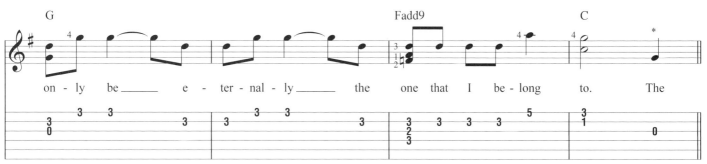

only be____ eternally____ the one that I belong to.____ The

*Sung one octave higher throughout **Chorus**.

Chorus

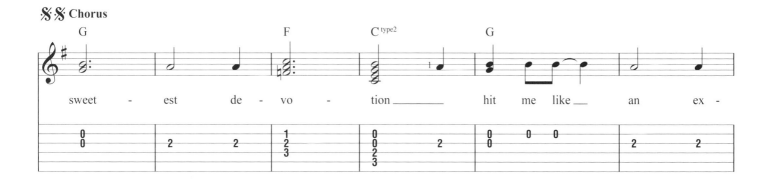

sweetest devotion____ hit me like an ex-

plosion.____ All of my____ life I've been frozen.____ The

3rd time, To Coda 2

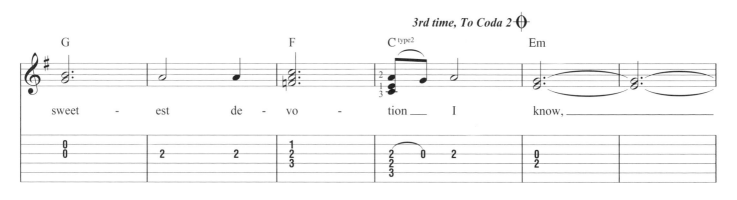

sweetest devotion____ I know,____

Interlude

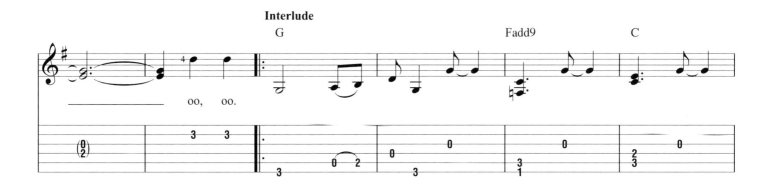

oo, oo.

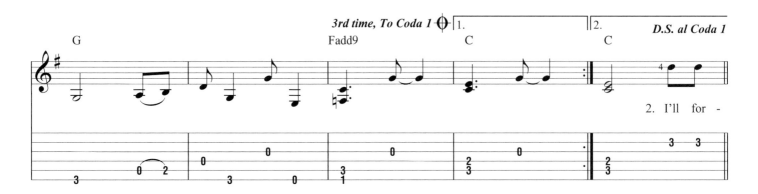

3rd time, To Coda 1 🎯 |1. |2. *D.S. al Coda 1*

2. I'll for -

🎯 **Coda 1**   **Bridge**

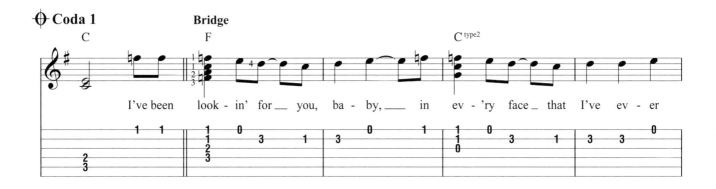

I've been look - in' for ___ you, baby, ___ in ev - 'ry face ___ that I've ev - er

known,   (Woo, hoo, oo, ___ hoo.) and there is   some - thin' 'bout ___ the   way   you   love

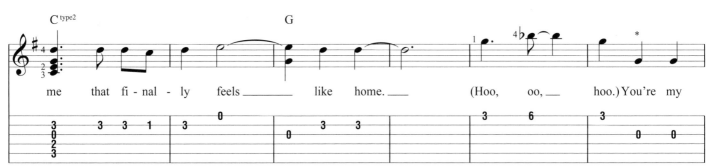

me   that   fi - nal - ly   feels _____ like   home. ___   (Hoo,   oo, ___   hoo.) You're   my

*Sung one octave higher.

44

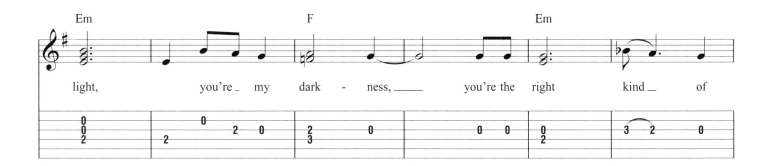

light, you're my dark - ness, ____ you're the right kind __ of

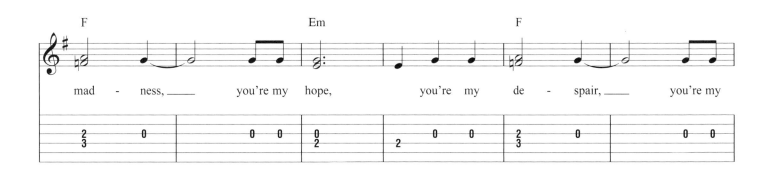

mad - ness, ____ you're my hope, you're my de - spair, ____ you're my

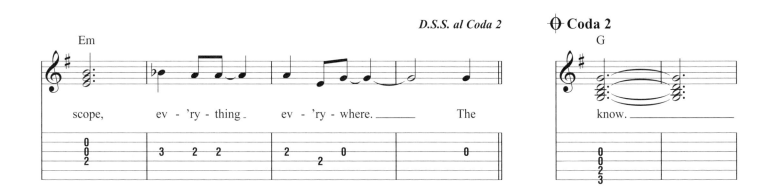

D.S.S. al Coda 2 Coda 2

scope, ev - 'ry - thing _ ev - 'ry - where. _____ The   know. _____

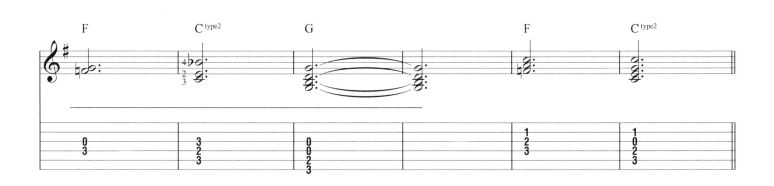

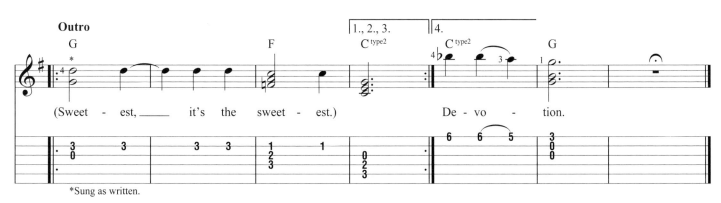

(Sweet - est, ____ it's the sweet - est.) De - vo - tion.

*Sung as written.

GUITAR PLAY-ALONG

This series will help you play your favorite songs quickly and easily. Just follow the tab and listen to the CD or online audio to hear how the guitar should sound, and then play along using the separate backing tracks. Playback tools are provided for slowing down the tempo without changing pitch and looping challenging parts. The melody and lyrics are included in the book so that you can sing or simply follow along.

80. ACOUSTIC ANTHOLOGY
00700175 Book/CD $19.95

81. ROCK ANTHOLOGY
00700176 Book/CD $22.99

82. EASY ROCK SONGS
00700177 Book/CD $12.99

83. THREE CHORD SONGS
00700178 Book/CD $16.99

84. STEELY DAN
00700200 Book/CD $16.99

85. THE POLICE
00700269 Book/CD $16.99

86. BOSTON
00700465 Book/CD $16.99

87. ACOUSTIC WOMEN
00700763 Book/CD $14.99

88. GRUNGE
00700467 Book/CD $16.99

89. REGGAE
00700468 Book/CD $15.99

90. CLASSICAL POP
00700469 Book/CD $14.99

91. BLUES INSTRUMENTALS
00700505 Book/CD $14.99

92. EARLY ROCK INSTRUMENTALS
00700506 Book/CD $14.99

93. ROCK INSTRUMENTALS
00700507 Book/CD $16.99

94. SLOW BLUES
00700508 Book/CD $16.99

95. BLUES CLASSICS
00700509 Book/CD $14.99

96. THIRD DAY
00700560 Book/CD $14.95

97. ROCK BAND
00700703 Book/CD $14.99

98. ROCK BAND
00700704 Book/CD $14.95

99. ZZ TOP
00700762 Book/CD $16.99

100. B.B. KING
00700466 Book/CD $16.99

101. SONGS FOR BEGINNERS
00701917 Book/CD $14.99

102. CLASSIC PUNK
00700769 Book/CD $14.99

103. SWITCHFOOT
00700773 Book/CD $16.99

104. DUANE ALLMAN
00700846 Book/CD $16.99

105. LATIN
00700939 Book/CD $16.99

106. WEEZER
00700958 Book/CD $14.99

107. CREAM
00701069 Book/CD $16.99

108. THE WHO
00701053 Book/CD $16.99

109. STEVE MILLER
00701054 Book/CD $14.99

110. SLIDE GUITAR HITS
00701055 Book/CD $16.99

111. JOHN MELLENCAMP
00701056 Book/CD $14.99

112. QUEEN
00701052 Book/CD $16.99

113. JIM CROCE
00701058 Book/CD $15.99

114. BON JOVI
00701060 Book/CD $14.99

115. JOHNNY CASH
00701070 Book/CD $16.99

116. THE VENTURES
00701124 Book/CD $14.99

117. BRAD PAISLEY
00701224 Book/CD $16.99

118. ERIC JOHNSON
00701353 Book/CD $16.99

119. AC/DC CLASSICS
00701356 Book/CD $17.99

120. PROGRESSIVE ROCK
00701457 Book/CD $14.99

121. U2
00701508 Book/CD $16.99

122. CROSBY, STILLS & NASH
00701610 Book/CD $16.99

123. LENNON & MCCARTNEY ACOUSTIC
00701614 Book/CD $16.99

124. MODERN WORSHIP
00701629 Book/CD $14.99

125. JEFF BECK
00701687 Book/CD $16.99

126. BOB MARLEY
00701701 Book/CD $16.99

127. 1970s ROCK
00701739 Book/CD $14.99

128. 1960s ROCK
00701740 Book/CD $14.99

129. MEGADETH
00701741 Book/CD $16.99

131. 1990s ROCK
00701743 Book/CD $14.99

132. COUNTRY ROCK
00701757 Book/CD $15.99

133. TAYLOR SWIFT
00701894 Book/CD $16.99

134. AVENGED SEVENFOLD
00701906 Book/CD $16.99

136. GUITAR THEMES
00701922 Book/CD $14.99

137. IRISH TUNES
00701966 Book/CD $15.99

138. BLUEGRASS CLASSICS
00701967 Book/CD $14.99

139. GARY MOORE
00702370 Book/CD $16.99

140. MORE STEVIE RAY VAUGHAN
00702396 Book/CD $17.99

141. ACOUSTIC HITS
00702401 Book/CD $16.99

143. SLASH
00702425 Book/Audio...........$19.99

144. DJANGO REINHARDT
00702531 Book/CD $16.99

145. DEF LEPPARD
00702532 Book/CD $16.99

146. ROBERT JOHNSON
00702533 Book/CD $16.99

147. SIMON & GARFUNKEL
14041591 Book/CD $16.99

148. BOB DYLAN
14041592 Book/CD $16.99

149. AC/DC HITS
14041593 Book/CD $17.99

150. ZAKK WYLDE
02501717 Book/CD $16.99

152. JOE BONAMASSA
02501751 Book/Audio...........$19.99

153. RED HOT CHILI PEPPERS
00702990 Book/CD $19.99

155. ERIC CLAPTON – FROM THE ALBUM *UNPLUGGED*
00703085 Book/CD $16.99

156. SLAYER
00703770 Book/CD $17.99

157. FLEETWOOD MAC
00101382 Book/CD $16.99

158. ULTIMATE CHRISTMAS
00101889 Book/CD $14.99

160. T-BONE WALKER
00102641 Book/CD $16.99

161. THE EAGLES – ACOUSTIC
00102659 Book/CD $17.99

162. THE EAGLES HITS
00102667 Book/CD $17.99

163. PANTERA
00103036 Book/CD $17.99

164. VAN HALEN 1986-1995
00110270 Book/CD $17.99

166. MODERN BLUES
00700764 Book/CD $16.99

167. DREAM THEATER
00111938 Book/2-CD $24.99

168. KISS
00113421 Book/CD $16.99

169. TAYLOR SWIFT
00115982 Book/CD $16.99

170. THREE DAYS GRACE
00117337 Book/CD $16.99

171. JAMES BROWN
00117420 Book/CD $16.99

173. TRANS-SIBERIAN ORCHESTRA
00119907 Book/CD $19.99

174. SCORPIONS
00122119 Book/CD $16.99

175. MICHAEL SCHENKER
00122127 Book/CD $16.99

176. BLUES BREAKERS WITH JOHN MAYALL & ERIC CLAPTON
00122132 Book/CD $19.99

177. ALBERT KING
00123271 Book/CD $16.99

178. JASON MRAZ
00124165 Book/CD $17.99

179. RAMONES
00127073 Book/CD $16.99

180. BRUNO MARS
00129706 Book/CD $16.99

181. JACK JOHNSON
00129854 Book/CD $16.99

182. SOUNDGARDEN
00138161 Book/Audio...........$17.99

184. KENNY WAYNE SHEPHERD
00138258 Book/Audio...........$17.99

187. JOHN DENVER
00140839 Book/Audio...........$17.99

EASY GUITAR WITH NOTES & TAB

This series features simplified arrangements with notes, tab, chord charts, and strum and pick patterns.

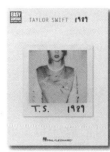

MIXED FOLIOS

00702287	Acoustic	$14.99
00702002	Acoustic Rock Hits for Easy Guitar	$12.95
00702166	All-Time Best Guitar Collection	$19.99
00699665	Beatles Best	$12.95
00702232	Best Acoustic Songs for Easy Guitar	$12.99
00119835	Best Children's Songs	$16.99
00702233	Best Hard Rock Songs	$14.99
00703055	The Big Book of Nursery Rhymes & Children's Songs	$14.99
00322179	The Big Easy Book of Classic Rock Guitar	$24.95
00698978	Big Christmas Collection	$16.95
00702394	Bluegrass Songs for Easy Guitar	$12.99
00703387	Celtic Classics	$14.99
00142539	Chart Hits of 2014-2015	$14.99
00702149	Children's Christian Songbook	$7.95
00702237	Christian Acoustic Favorites	$12.95
00702028	Christmas Classics	$7.95
00101779	Christmas Guitar	$14.99
00702185	Christmas Hits	$9.95
00702141	Classic Rock	$8.95
00702203	CMT's 100 Greatest Country Songs	$27.95
00702283	The Contemporary Christian Collection	$16.99
00702006	Contemporary Christian Favorites	$9.95
00702239	Country Classics for Easy Guitar	$19.99
00702282	Country Hits of 2009–2010	$14.99
00702085	Disney Movie Hits	$12.95
00702257	Easy Acoustic Guitar Songs	$14.99
00702280	Easy Guitar Tab White Pages	$29.99
00702212	Essential Christmas	$9.95
00702041	Favorite Hymns for Easy Guitar	$9.95
00702281	4 Chord Rock	$9.99
00126894	Frozen	$14.99
00702286	Glee	$16.99
00699374	Gospel Favorites	$14.95
00122138	The Grammy Awards® Record of the Year 1958-2011	$19.99
00702160	The Great American Country Songbook	$15.99
00702050	Great Classical Themes for Easy Guitar	$6.95
00702116	Greatest Hymns for Guitar	$8.95
00702130	The Groovy Years	$9.95
00702184	Guitar Instrumentals	$9.95
00148030	Halloween Guitar Songs	$14.99
00702273	Irish Songs	$12.99
00702275	Jazz Favorites for Easy Guitar	$14.99
00702274	Jazz Standards for Easy Guitar	$14.99
00702162	Jumbo Easy Guitar Songbook	$19.95
00702258	Legends of Rock	$14.99
00702261	Modern Worship Hits	$14.99
00702189	MTV's 100 Greatest Pop Songs	$24.95
00702272	1950s Rock	$14.99
00702271	1960s Rock	$14.99
00702270	1970s Rock	$14.99
00702269	1980s Rock	$14.99
00702268	1990s Rock	$14.99
00109725	Once	$14.99
00702187	Selections from O Brother Where Art Thou?	$12.95
00702178	100 Songs for Kids	$14.99
00702515	Pirates of the Caribbean	$12.99
00702125	Praise and Worship for Guitar	$9.95
00702155	Rock Hits for Guitar	$9.95
00702285	Southern Rock Hits	$12.99
00702866	Theme Music	$12.99
00121535	30 Easy Celtic Guitar Solos	$14.99
00702220	Today's Country Hits	$9.95
00702198	Today's Hits for Guitar	$9.95
00121900	Today's Women of Pop & Rock	$14.99
00702217	Top Christian Hits	$12.95
00103626	Top Hits of 2012	$14.99
00702294	Top Worship Hits	$14.99
00702206	Very Best of Rock	$9.95
00702255	VH1's 100 Greatest Hard Rock Songs	$27.95
00702175	VH1's 100 Greatest Songs of Rock and Roll	$24.95
00702253	Wicked	$12.99

ARTIST COLLECTIONS

00702267	AC/DC for Easy Guitar	$15.99
00702598	Adele for Easy Guitar	$14.99
00702001	Best of Aerosmith	$16.95
00702040	Best of the Allman Brothers	$14.99
00702865	J.S. Bach for Easy Guitar	$12.99
00702169	Best of The Beach Boys	$12.99
00702292	The Beatles — 1	$19.99
00125796	Best of Chuck Berry	$14.99
00702201	The Essential Black Sabbath	$12.95
02501615	Zac Brown Band — The Foundation	$16.99
02501621	Zac Brown Band — You Get What You Give	$16.99
00702043	Best of Johnny Cash	$16.99
00702291	Very Best of Coldplay	$12.99
00702263	Best of Casting Crowns	$12.99
00702090	Eric Clapton's Best	$10.95
00702086	Eric Clapton — from the Album Unplugged	$10.95
00702202	The Essential Eric Clapton	$12.95
00702250	blink-182 — Greatest Hits	$12.99
00702053	Best of Patsy Cline	$10.95
00702229	The Very Best of Creedence Clearwater Revival	$14.99
00702145	Best of Jim Croce	$14.99
00702278	Crosby, Stills & Nash	$12.99
00702219	David Crowder*Band Collection	$12.95
14042809	Bob Dylan	$14.99
00702276	Fleetwood Mac — Easy Guitar Collection	$14.99
00130952	Foo Fighters	$14.99
00139462	The Very Best of Grateful Dead	$14.99
00702136	Best of Merle Haggard	$12.99
00702227	Jimi Hendrix — Smash Hits	$14.99
00702288	Best of Hillsong United	$12.99
00702236	Best of Antonio Carlos Jobim	$12.95
00702245	Elton John — Greatest Hits 1970–2002	$14.99
00129855	Jack Johnson	$14.99
00702204	Robert Johnson	$10.99
00702234	Selections from Toby Keith — 35 Biggest Hits	$12.95
00702003	Kiss	$9.95
00110578	Best of Kutless	$12.99
00702216	Lynyrd Skynyrd	$15.99
00702182	The Essential Bob Marley	$12.95
00146081	Maroon 5	$14.99
00702346	Bruno Mars — Doo-Wops & Hooligans	$12.99
00121925	Bruno Mars – Unorthodox Jukebox	$12.99
00702248	Paul McCartney — All the Best	$14.99
00702129	Songs of Sarah McLachlan	$12.95
00125484	The Best of MercyMe	$12.99
02501316	Metallica — Death Magnetic	$15.95
00702209	Steve Miller Band — Young Hearts (Greatest Hits)	$12.95
00124167	Jason Mraz	$14.99
00702096	Best of Nirvana	$14.99
00702211	The Offspring — Greatest Hits	$12.95
00138026	One Direction	$14.99
00702030	Best of Roy Orbison	$12.95
00702144	Best of Ozzy Osbourne	$14.99
00702279	Tom Petty	$12.99
00102911	Pink Floyd	$16.99
00702139	Elvis Country Favorites	$9.95
00702293	The Very Best of Prince	$12.99
00699415	Best of Queen for Guitar	$14.99
00109279	Best of R.E.M.	$14.99
00702208	Red Hot Chili Peppers — Greatest Hits	$12.95
00702093	Rolling Stones Collection	$17.95
00702196	Best of Bob Seger	$12.95
00146046	Ed Sheeran	$14.99
00702252	Frank Sinatra — Nothing But the Best	$12.99
00702010	Best of Rod Stewart	$14.95
00702049	Best of George Strait	$12.95
00702259	Taylor Swift for Easy Guitar	$14.99
00702260	Taylor Swift — Fearless	$12.99
00139727	Taylor Swift — 1989	$17.99
00115960	Taylor Swift — Red	$16.99
00702290	Taylor Swift — Speak Now	$15.99
00702262	Chris Tomlin Collection	$14.99
00702226	Chris Tomlin — See the Morning	$12.95
00148643	Train	$14.99
00702427	U2 — 18 Singles	$14.99
00102711	Van Halen	$16.99
00702108	Best of Stevie Ray Vaughan	$10.95
00702123	Best of Hank Williams	$12.99
00702111	Stevie Wonder — Guitar Collection	$9.95
00702228	Neil Young — Greatest Hits	$15.99
00119133	Neil Young — Harvest	$14.99
00702188	Essential ZZ Top	$10.95

Prices, contents and availability subject to change without notice.

HAL•LEONARD® CORPORATION

7777 W. BLUEMOUND RD. P.O. BOX 13819 MILWAUKEE, WI 53213

Visit Hal Leonard online at
www.halleonard.com

1015